Want a Better Life

Annie P. Jones

Want a Better Life

Annie P. Jones

LOWBAR
PUBLISHING COMPANY

905 South Douglas Avenue • Nashville, Tennessee 37204
Phone: 615-972-2842
E-mail: Lowbarpublishingcompany@gmail.com
Web site: www.Lowbarbookstore.com

Copyright © 2018 Annie P. Jones

No part of this book may be reproduced or transmitted in any form or by any means—graphic, electronic, or mechanical, including photocopying, recording, taping, or by any information storage retrieval system—without the permission, in writing, of the publisher or author.

Lowbar Publishing Company 905 S. Douglas Ave.
Nashville, Tennessee 37204
615-972-2842

Lowbarpublishingcompany@gmail.com
www.Lowbarbookstore.com

Content Editor: Calvin C. Barlow, Jr.
Editor: Michelle
Graphic and Cover Design Artist: Alishaa

Printed in the United States of America. Nashville, Tennessee

ISBN: 978-1-7329202-1-7

For additional information or to contact the author for workshops or seminars, please email the author at Jonesladyapj@gmail.com or Lowbar Publishing Company.

Scripture quotes are taken from the King James Version unless otherwise stated.

Table of Contents

Foreword vi

Dedication vii

Acknowledgments viii

Chapter 1: Get A Better Life Right Here
And Right Now Get A Better Life 1

Chapter 2: Authority Dominion And Power 10

Chapter 3: Don't Take Anyone For Granted 18

Chapter 4: The Bible 26

Chapter 5: Watch God Provide 34

Chapter 6: God's Power, Promise, And Purpose ... 47

Chapter 7: Wait On The Lord 61

Chapter 8: Want More Do More 69

About The Author 79

Foreword

WANT A BETTER LIFE? Read this book; it is very encouraging and inspiring. Life is always throwing challenges, choices, changes, and decisions after decisions at us. These issues can cause burdens, depression, heartaches, and more.

This book tells us that no matter what the problem may be, we can always seek God. Because He is willing and waiting to carry us through.

Melinda Williams

Special Education Teacher

San Antonio, Texas

Dedication

I dedicate this book to my mother, Melzina Townes. She is my rock. She taught me that I could do all things through Christ who strengthens me.

Acknowledgments

I would like to acknowledge my father, the late Henry B. Townes. I always knew my parents were there for me, no matter what I was going through. They taught me that due diligence and hard work would pay off. They instilled in me the courage to keep God first and foremost in my life. And it has helped me to endure many challenging situations throughout my life.

I would like to thank my family, especially my sisters and brothers. Your support means so much to me. I really appreciate all of my friends who encouraged me to finish this book. My hope is that it inspires others who are struggling with their dreams and goals. Keep pressing forward and remember to enjoy each moment!

Chapter 1

GET A BETTER LIFE RIGHT HERE AND RIGHT NOW GET A BETTER LIFE

Do you want a better life right here and right now? I believe we have been given the power to do just that. *"The earth is the Lord's and the fulness thereof; the world, and they that dwell therein,"* Psalm 24:1. This means everything belongs to God including us. The environment was created for mankind. I believe that He wants us to enjoy His goodness and His creation. Many times, we are so busy that we fail to partake of His wonderful blessings. For example, when was the last time you stopped to embrace the simple pleasures of life? Walking in the sun, the rain or the cold. Talking to an old friend or a stranger. These things do not cost you anything. But they can bring you and others so much joy.

Our lives are so busy and filled with technology. We do not take the time to really enjoy one another. We need to stop and turn off our devices and have a good conversation. Email, Facebook, Instagram, Snapchat, and Twitter will still be available whenever we choose to use them. On the other hand, we only have a limited amount of time to spend with one another.

We should use it wisely. Decide what is truly important and make that your top priority. We can spend more time with our spouses, friends, and families. If we do not do it now, we may regret it later.

I have been told that I am pre-diabetic. I was advised to lose twenty pounds. I have decided to make this a priority. I have an invitation to a luncheon on Saturday. I have made plans to attend a free tennis clinic instead. I need to lose weight. Therefore, my choice is clear. I asked myself, "Which of these activities will give me the most benefits?" I need to focus on movement. Sitting and eating are part of what got me in this condition. I must change my behavior. My community has a bike riding club. I plan to join the club. I have given myself three months to lose the twenty pounds.

Change is necessary to accomplish any goal. I realize things do not magically happen. You must make decisions and execute them. Otherwise, things will remain the same or get worse. Many people sit around moping and complaining. They fail to act to change their situations. Let me assure you that moaning, and groaning cannot change your life. You must become an active participant in order to see your desired results. My former pastor, Reverend Doctor Jim Holley, used to say, "God does not do anything in our lives unless we participate." I truly believe this.

For instance, if you have a great idea, you must take the necessary steps to bring it to life. There have been times that I have had a great idea. But I did not do the work to make it a reality. God gave it to someone else, and they had major success with it. I'm sure that I am not the only one this has happened to. Read Matthew 25: 14-28! This is the story about the man who was given one talent, but he hid it. This talent was taken from him and given to the man who had ten. This story was referring to money. This may also apply to our personal talents. The moral of the story is that we must use whatever talent we possess for the good of mankind. Failing to do this will result in grave consequences.

God has given us authority, dominion, and power to live a better life right here and now. Many times, we fail to utilize the talents God has given us. We make excuses because we do not want to do the work. First, you must decide that you really want a better life. Next, you must start doing the work to make it happen. There are many stories of people, who started out with almost nothing and ended up rich and successful. Anyway, if you read their stories, you would discover they had many disappointments and struggles. You would find that they worked hard and did not give up. They believed in themselves. So, can you start today? Do not put it off!

I believe God wants us to enjoy all aspects of our lives. When Jesus was here, He did not spend all His time in the synagogue. He did many things; He talked to strangers. He performed miracles. He turned water into wine while attending a wedding according to John 2: 1-11. He went to people's homes. He took advantage of all the various things which were available here on earth. Some people are totally focused on a single area of their life; they hardly take time to enjoy other aspects which are available.

God has allowed us to create and invent many things. I believe He wants us to enjoy all of these inventions. All things have a time and place. Ecclesiastes 3:1 states, *"To everything there is a season, and a time, to every purpose under the heaven."* I believe God wants us to have a balanced life. He wants us to embrace all the wonders of the earth. He created them with us in mind. What a mighty and wonderful God we serve!

CHANGE

According to Webster, the definition of change is to make different or to transform, moving in a different direction. Choosing a different course, direction, or position. Undergoing loss or modification. A good example might be to lose weight. You must make changes. Also, you must change directions to get from one place to another. Changing your hairstyle is a form of modification. Anyway, you get the idea!

People by nature do not like change, but we cannot stop it. Change is always happening, from the moment of conception until death. Our bodies are always changing. We must adapt to different stages of life. Transformation is a natural part of life. Nothing and no one stays the same.

The world is constantly changing. We must learn new things. Our response is usually, "I like doing it the old way." Why did it have to change? Most of us are guilty of this type of thinking. We do not like to move out of our comfort zones. For example, in the workplace, change often involves dealing with technology. Therefore, we must move in a different direction. Here is some good news! The brain has the capacity to learn new things at any age. The more you use it, the better it gets. Data and research support this fact.

CHANGE: MAKE IT; BE IT; SEE IT

Most of us want some type of change in our lives. Perhaps you are wondering, "How can I make that happen?" First, you must make a decision about what you want. Next, you have to be the change. This means making it a part of your being. You must see the change --- actually envision it. See a picture of the change in your mind's eye. For example, let's say you want to lose weight. First, you have to make a decision to change your eating habits. Know that this will not happen immediately. You may need to change your thinking. Take time to exercise, eat healthily, get enough sleep, and drink enough water. Do not make excuses, simply do it. Tell yourself; "I am worth it." I must take better care of myself. Remember if you do not, others will follow suit. You must value yourself. Generally, others will not think more of you than you think of yourself.

We are in charge of ourselves. This includes our time and money. This is very important. We have a limited amount of time on this planet. We need to use it wisely. Do you plan to be successful? You must be in control of all your assets. Choosing not to control these things allows someone else to take advantage of you. People have asked me, "What are you doing?" They were not interested in my answer. They only wanted to tell me what they wanted me to do. They had no consideration for my aspirations or time. God has given all of us a choice and a voice. We must take responsibility for ourselves.

CREATIVE PROBLEM SOLVER

Sometimes we are forced to change our thinking. For example, I know that I am pre-diabetic. Recently, I was told that I should limit sugar and fried foods. This would help me lose weight. Immediately, I started craving foods that I needed to avoid. Should I give in to the cravings, or should I make healthier choices? I had a conversation with a neighbor. We discussed health concerns. Also, we talked about the foods we could not have. I told him suddenly that I wanted spaghetti. I mentioned a chicken burger, which I liked. He answered, "Why not use that in the spaghetti?" This was a great idea. He added, "We must find new ways to cheat. We must change the way we think about food. I can still have desserts and pasta. I must find healthy solutions."

We were created to be problem solvers. I believe the trials we encounter in life help us to solve problems. We are forced to do things differently. Life is such an adventure with new possibilities every day. Maybe I will author a healthy cookbook. What an exciting idea. I like to cook and try new recipes. This will be a fun project. Changing my thinking about eating healthily has given me a new perspective. I dare say this is a good approach for any problem one may encounter. Remember, do not dwell on how big your problems are. Just know that God is bigger than all of your problems. He is able, availably ready, and willing to help us any time. We must ask Him. My pastor, Reverend Doctor Larry Jordan, once did a sermon, "When in Doubt, Don't Leave God Out."

There is no need to struggle with difficult situations. *"God is our refuge and strength, a very present help in trouble,"* Psalm 46:1. He is always available. What a valuable resource! We can call on Him any time; day or night. He is never too busy to listen. You will never receive a busy signal or the wrong advice. You can trust Him with your entire life. Also, you will never have to worry about getting an unexpected bill. What could be better than that? There is no one like Him. There is a song, "What a Friend We Have in Jesus." *"Oh, what needless pains we bear all because we do not carry everything to God in prayer"*. Try this strategy; you will get amazing results. Prayer is a very valuable tool. Use it often and freely!

Prayer is definitely the key to overcoming difficult problems. 2nd Chronicles 7:14 says, *"If my people, which are called by my name, shall humble themselves, and pray, and seek my face, and turn from their wicked ways; then will I hear from heaven, and forgive their sin, and will heal their land."* Many times, when we encounter problems, we try to handle them on our own. Usually, this is not the best way. After things fall apart, when we exhaust all possible options, as a last resort, we ask God for help. Matthew 6:33 states; "But seek ye first the kingdom of God, and his righteousness; and all these things shall be added unto you." So instead of asking God last, we should consult Him first. I can assure you of a much better outcome. Whatever I am attempting to do, I consult Him first. Whenever there seems to be no answer, just start praying. Step back, take a deep breath and wait for God to respond. You will be quite pleased. Tap into God's awesome power. You will not regret it! What changes do you need to address in your life? Remember it is important to write your thoughts down because this will create a roadmap for you to follow. Just thinking about it is okay. Writing it down will cause it to become a reality.

NOTES:

_____

_____

_____

_____

_____

_____

_____

_____

_____

_____

_____

_____

Chapter 2

AUTHORITY DOMINION AND POWER

We have been given authority, dominion, and power over the earth. Genesis 1:26 states, "And God said, let us make man in our image, after our likeness: and let them have dominion over the fish of the sea, and over the fowl of the air, and over the cattle, and over all the earth, and over every creeping thing that creepeth upon the earth." Therefore, take charge of your destiny. Step boldly into it. Do not stop chasing your dreams. Believe that you are destined to be great. God created us in His image. He expects greatness from us. That is His plan for our lives. We have the responsibility to fulfill our purpose. We have all been given certain abilities and talents. So, get busy doing what you were meant to do. Develop and maximize your potential. Preparation is a necessary part of the process. Set small goals and celebrate each victory. Each achievement will prepare you for bigger and better things. You will marvel at your success as you reach greater heights.

You will get new ideas from others. Networking is a great tool. Use it to increase your marketing ability. There are many local chapters you can join. Just google the area that you are interested in. Your local Chamber of Commerce is a good place to start. Once you make a commitment, God will put the right people in your path to help you get to the next level. You will be astonished at how this works.

For example, I am working on launching a scarf product. My sister gave me the idea of making scarves for the college football season. She suggested using the college colors. Right after she told me this, another friend told me that she had done this on a small scale with friends from her exercise club. I am excited to use this idea on a larger scale. Perhaps, I may get to the NFL. What an enormous opportunity. My goal is to end up on Shark Tank to pitch my idea. "They say that if your dream does not scare you, it is not big enough." Go for the gusto, what do you have to lose? Many people have started with almost nothing and ended up with great success. Why not you or me?

THINKING ABOUT IT IS HARDER THAN DOING IT

Sometimes we have to stop thinking and start doing the work. You have to give yourself a deadline. Otherwise, you will keep thinking; I will do it later. Looking at the big picture can be overwhelming. Try breaking things down into small manageable steps. Devote specific time for your project. Do your best to stick to it. Decide to start now! For example, cleaning my closet seemed to be too much. Finally, I decided to get started. Once I started, I marveled at the progress; it was such a great relief. I was able to keep going. A good outcome will motivate you to do more. You want to see the finished product.

Suddenly, your thinking will change. I can do this. I am capable. I will succeed. You can use this confidence in all areas of your life. Believing that you can is a big part of the plan. I believe God wants us to have a better life right here and now! Yes, we must actually do the work. The benefits and rewards are so worth it. Do whatever is necessary to start the process.

Accomplishing your goals will enrich your life; forge ahead and expand your horizons. You will enjoy your journey, just as it is meant to be. Things do not stay the same. We are designed to adapt to change. Learning new things can add great experiences. Yes, it may be hard to step outside of your comfort zone, but it can help you get to the next level. Your life will be enhanced, along with the people you interact with. The beauty of life is that we do not know what the future holds. We do know that God is already there, and He wants the best for us. All we must do is tap into His magnificent power and expect wonderful results.

Concentrate on all your wonderful assets and watch them increase. The more you use them, the better they will become. We all have unlimited possibilities. Stop allowing them to go unused. Start thinking of ways to reach your full potential. Our creator wants us to have the best of everything. He has put everything in place to ensure our success. According to His word, He will not withhold any good thing from the upright. Psalm 84:11 states, *"For the Lord God is a sun and shield: The Lord will give grace and glory: no good thing will he withhold from them that walk uprightly."* I have found that if I want to get more, I must give more. We cannot beat God n giving. When I least expect it, I get unexpected rewards. Try this and experience His goodness and grace. There is nothing better!

FOCUS ON YOUR GOALS

As the saying goes, "Reach for the moon; you will land among the stars." I believe we can all be successful right here and now. We must make that choice. We are all good at something. We need to take advantage of whatever that is. According to Doctor John F. Demartini, author and educator, "Whatever we think about and thank about we bring about." Our thought process has far-reaching effects. Be careful what you think for it will likely come true. Remember you are in control of your thoughts. Dwell on positive things. Do not drift into negative territories. Make a point of stopping those thoughts in their tracks. "Energy flows where attention goes," says Dr. Michael Beckwith. Whatever you decide to spend your time and energy on is what will become a reality for you. So why not focus on your dreams and goals. Watching them come to life is such a rewarding experience.

Do not get upset when things don't go the way you expect. Think of yourself as a creative problem solver. We all get stuck sometimes. How we choose to manage a given situation can change the outcome. A problem may cause you to sweat. Think of it as a way to allow your inner glow to shine. Life can present some overwhelming moments. Remember that God is bigger than whatever we are facing. God can help you to overcome all obstacles.

Stay focused on your objective. Try different approaches. Maybe your current practice is not working. Do not be afraid to think outside of the box. Ask others for help. They may be able to offer you a different viewpoint. Tap into whatever resources that are available. Exhaust all possible options. Believe that you will have a successful outcome. Keep an open mind. You may need to adjust and change your original plan. Do not lose sight of your goals. Decide to do whatever is necessary to accomplish them. There is a song that says, we fall down, but we get back up again. God is full of mercy and grace. Therefore, we are able to continue. Even if you get off track, review your plans and keep going. Do not allow anything to stop you.

CHOOSE TO THRIVE AND NOT JUST SURVIVE

Do you really want a better life? Making good choices is how it starts. God has given us authority, dominion, and power. Take control and responsibility for your actions. We all make mistakes. Learn from them and vow to do better. Refuse to allow that to stop your progress. Never lose sight of your goals. Keep your eyes on where you are trying to go. Remind yourself that you are capable. Believe that success is possible. Ultimately you will eventually reach your destination. Think of the benefits you will savor. One step at a time! And remember to enjoy your journey. Once you reach your destination, it will not matter how long it took you to get there. For example, maybe you wanted to get a four-year degree. Perhaps it took you a lot longer than you expected. No one will ask you, why did it take so long? The fact that you finally got it is what matters. Hard work and determination will pay off.

John 10:10 states, *"The thief cometh not, but for to steal, and to kill, and to destroy: I am come that they may might have life, and that they might have it more abundantly."."* Therefore, God wants us to have a good and prosperous life. That is a part of the reason why Christ came. What must we do in order to obtain this blessing? Romans 10:10 states, *"For with the heart man believeth unto righteousness; and with the mouth confession is made unto salvation."* This is what we are required to do. Do you want an abundant life? This is a step in the right direction. Maybe you want to work for a major corporation. You have to accept and abide by their rules. The same principle applies here.

According to the English Oxford dictionaries, blessing is God's favor and protection. God is bigger than what we can comprehend. Just getting money and things is not all that it includes. Favor and protection go beyond material things. According to Google, favor is an attitude of approval or liking. Mental and physical health are included. These are things that money cannot buy. He protects us from dangers that we may not be aware of. All things are possible with God. While we may not have everything that we want. He has promised to supply all of our needs according to His riches and glory by Christ Jesus, according to Philippians 4:19. A relationship with Him guarantees us access to whatever we need; whenever we need it. No one else can offer us that.

WE DON'T KNOW OUR OWN STRENGTH

Many times, we do not realize how strong we are. Sometimes we have to deal with difficult situations. We really do not know how much we can bear. Somehow, we get through it, and we are stronger than before. 2nd Corinthians 12:9 teaches that God's grace is enough for us. *"And he said to me, my grace is sufficient for thee. for my strength is made perfect in weakness. Most gladly therefore will I rather glory in my infirmities, that the power of Christ may rest upon me."* This is a powerful force. We do not have to handle anything alone. Life is designed to encounter adversity. How we choose to handle problems truly makes a difference. Whenever you have trials, go to the scriptures. You will find something to help you get past the difficulty. God has promised never to leave or forsake us. We can stand on His word; it will never fail us. What is your approach to dealing with overwhelming, challenging encounters? Do you go to the phone for help? There is a saying that says, "It is better to go to the throne." I have found this to be very true. No matter what the problem may be, God has the answer! What do you need to focus on? What should be your main priority now?

NOTES:

Chapter 3

Don't Take Anyone For Granted

Never take anyone for granted. When they are no longer here, you will realize how much they mean to you. Most of us have planned to call or visit someone. We receive a call, telling us that they are gone. We wish we had carried out the plan. Now, we realize it is too late. There is no way to change what has happened. We must deal with the loss. Start today, tell your friends and family how much they mean to you. Most of all, tell God also because He is the provider of all things. Make a habit of talking to Him daily. Do not wait until you have a problem that you cannot solve. Your life will work so much better.

Friends and family are precious and valuable. We should treasure them. Once they are gone, they cannot be replaced. Schedule time to create great memories. Remember we can enjoy many moments in life together. Do not allow the various opportunities to pass you by. Be sure to give the people in your life a priority status. You will be glad that you did.

STRESSING DOESN'T HELP

Dealing with stress is not an easy task. However, it can be managed. We all encounter difficult challenges. Here are some physical things you can try: Yoga and deep breathing are helpful and good for you. This will calm you down. Think pleasant thoughts. An example might be a good vacation. Mentally, plan your next getaway. Listen to music; it will soothe you. Biking, shopping, and walking are excellent choices. Go to a movie, connect with friends. Get a massage, a manicure, and a pedicure. Put your feet up and relax. Prayer and meditation are great spiritual tools. They help you remind yourself that you are not alone. God is always there. He will guide you through any situation. As the song says, while you're trying to figure it out, He has already worked it out. Discussing it with someone that you trust can be helpful. Ask others for help. Networking and social media can be helpful. This is a good way to find out how others are coping. There is a saying; "Learn from the mistakes of others, because you don't have time to make all of them yourself."

Life is full of unplanned events. Sometimes it seems that everything just goes wrong. There is a saying; "God will not bring you to it if He cannot see you through it." There is a song by Brian Courtney Wilson with the words; "No matter how deep you are in despair, He will never leave you there." Our trials do help to make us stronger. Life has a way of knocking us down. Managing difficult situations helps to build character. There are many stories of how people have used challenging encounters to propel themselves to the next level. Figuring out how to overcome life's problems can be very rewarding. We are designed to overcome adversity. This is how good ideas come to life. Keep pressing toward your goals. Romans 8: 37states, *"Nay, in all these things we are more than conquerors through him that loved us."*

THE DEVIL IN A PAPER BAG

Do you know people who are always ready to point out what is wrong? They are never positive. Whatever you say, they tell you how it is not going to work. That is one way the devil tries to stop you from reaching your full potential. However, when you point out something negative, which they say, they are quick to point out that it is not what they mean. You just interpreted it wrong. They will never admit their mistakes. Once you have successfully executed your idea, they will go around, telling people how they supported you. The reality is that the opposite is true. The devil will gladly take credit for your success. After he has failed to stop you. God has given us the discretion to recognize his tactics. You must stay focused to complete your goals. Refuse to listen to the nay Sayers! Seek out those who are positive and supportive.

Do not allow the devil to put you into a paper bag. He will seal it tight, and you will have a hard time getting out. Stay focused on your goals. Work hard at reaching your destination. Don't allow anyone to put you in the devil's paper bag.

COPYING AND PASTING

While you do not need to reinvent the wheel, you may be able to take an idea and execute it in a different way. Many have gained success in this manner. For example, Walmart took Kmart's model to the southern region of the United States and gained great success. Many times, this works. However, do not be afraid to trust your own instincts. Sometimes you will get a good idea. Do not let doubt and fear stop you from using it. I have failed to do this in the past. Later, I found that someone else had capitalized on my exact idea. You must seize the moment. Do not miss out on a valuable opportunity.

Develop a plan of action and move forward. Hard work and preparation are necessary to complete the job. Achieving what you started out to do is a wonderful thing. This makes the process worthwhile. God really wants us to live our best lives right here and now. There are so many possibilities. We are fortunate to live in a country that allows us to continue to expand our horizons. Do not allow anyone to stop you from reaching your goals. Do not wait; start now!

We are designed to be problem solvers. You may come across problems in your everyday happenstances. Remember, you are not the only one experiencing problems. Coming up with a solution can yield tremendous results. People will pay for good products. We all have talents and abilities. Do not fail to utilize your talents and abilities. Get busy and start changing your life!

THERE IS NO LIMIT

There is a song by Israel entitled; "There is no limit when God is in it." You will find this to be true as you strive to reach your true potential. You will get many new ideas. There is a scripture, Malachi 3:10, that states, *"Bring ye all the tithes into the storehouse, that there may be meat in mine house, and prove me now herewith, saith the Lord of hosts, if I will not open you the windows of heaven, and pour you out a blessing that there shall not be room enough to receive it."* This is referring to tithing, giving ten percent of your earnings to the church will yield you positive results. Do not knock it until you have tried it. I believe there are unlimited blessings in store for each of us. Often, we fail to tap into whatever means that are available. Maybe what you are doing is not working, then try this. This is not my promise; it is God's word. He always keeps His word.

Lamentations 3:22-23 states, *"It is of the Lord's mercies that we are not consumed, because his compassions fail not. They are new every morning: great is thy faithfulness."* This scripture tells us how compassionate and merciful God is. Every day, He gives us another chance to do great things. He is a God of many chances. We have the responsibility to take advantage of His wonderful opportunities. Do not waste time complaining. Learn to be grateful and thank Him for everything. Sometimes, I get the urge to complain, and then I will remember to thank Him for all of my accomplishments. You cannot complain and be thankful at the same time.

God has a purpose and a plan for each of us. Our assignments are not the same. We have unique abilities and talents.

Sometimes they intersect. Therefore, we may be able to help others on the way to our destination. Working together is a good thing. Everyone has the burden of fulfilling what they have been called to do. Do not waste time competing and comparing. Stay focused on your goals. This will give you a good measure of relief from anxiety without medication. We can all be great according to His purpose for our lives. There is no room for envy or jealousy. All of us can be successful in our own right. That is His divine will for us. Once you hit upon a solution to a problem, remember the blessing is meant to be shared. This will bring about greater blessings to you. You will be overjoyed to discover how this works. Make a decision to partake of God's wonderful grace and mercy.

All of us have setbacks; however, our trials serve to make us stronger and more resilient. Usually, there is a blessing on the other side of whatever you are going through. There is a song by Travis Greene, "You Made a Way." Here are some of the lyrics; *"When our backs were against the wall, and it looked as if it was over, you made a way. Don't know how but you did it. And we are standing here only because you made a way. Holding on to faith you know that"* … He will never leave or forsake you. He will deliver you. So, never give up. As the song goes, trust and believe, my friend. He will work it out for you. You may be thinking that this sounds too good to be true. Believe me! It is that simple! Sometimes we make life more complicated than it is. Vow to start your journey today!

Once you make the decision, your subconscious will start to generate ideas to help you get wherever you are trying to go. Psalm 139:14 states, *"I will praise thee; for I am fearfully and wonderfully made: marvelous are thy works; and that my soul knoweth right well."* Most of us waste a lot of time trying to fix what is already fixed. We have been designed to carry out his divine plan. All we must do is follow the blueprint. Just because things do not turn out the way we expect is not a cause for alarm.

As I look back over my life, some of my best blessings happened when I did not get what I thought I wanted. God always anticipates exactly what we need. Once I discovered this fact, I stopped getting upset over things that did not go my way. I came to the realization that life might not be perfect, but it was still good. So, I have decided to enjoy each moment that I am given. Are you dealing with anxiety problems, and stress in your life? Try focusing on your goals and your purpose.

NOTES:

Chapter 4

THE BIBLE

There is a saying: *"The Bible stands for the best instruction before leaving earth."* Our forefathers followed the scriptures because they did not have all of the options we have available today. The Bible offers solutions to all the problems that we can possibly envision. Often, we choose other options, since they are readily available. Don't get me wrong; technology is a wonderful tool. Do not forget that God is the one who has allowed us to invent this option. Sometimes we fail to realize it is not meant to replace His word. I think that we all agree that technology is a good thing. God has created everything with us in mind. He has given us dominion over the earth.

Still, He wants us to lean and depend on Him. John 15:5 states, *"I am the vine, ye are the branches: He that abideth in me, and I in him, the same bringeth forth much fruit: for without me ye can do nothing."* He wants us to put Him first. A lot of times we use Him as a last resort. After we have tried everything else, and it does not work. Finally, we decide to try God. I have found that reversing this process is a much better option. Do you want to reduce anxiety and stress in your life? This is truly a better solution.

A FRESH PERSPECTIVE

I have found that sometimes I ponder over a problem. What is the right decision? Somehow, I seem unable to come up with it. I pray and go to bed. After a good night's sleep, I wake up with the answer. Prayer really does change things. We are truly given new mercies every day. I had worked on something all day. I failed to get it resolved. The next day, I got up and magically I had it done. Many times, it may not happen in the time that you expect it. Sometimes we just must wait. We must trust God and give Him time. Isaiah 40:31 states, *"But they that wait upon the Lord shall mount up with wings as eagles; they shall run, and not be weary; and they shall walk, and not faint."*

Yolanda Adams has a song that says, *"It's already all right now"*. No matter what the problem is, He has the answer. Sometimes we have to just let it simmer before God gives us the answer. Hence the adage, "Take an aspirin and call me in the morning." Think of prayer as the aspirin. Most of the time you will not have to call God in the morning. Suddenly the answer is revealed to you. I don't know how to explain this. I do know that it is thrilling how it works. There is a song that says we will understand it better by and by.

THERE IS NO QUICK FIX

As Americans, we live in a society that wants a quick fix for everything. While in some cases that may be possible. Most of the time, that is not how it works. You will have to be patient and persistent to reach your personal goals. Study other successful people. You will find that they endured many failures before they got a successful outcome. One example that comes to mind is President Abraham Lincoln; he did not become president overnight. He went through many hard trials and tribulations before he finally reached his goal. You must stay focused. Do not lose sight of your dreams. Believe that you can! There is a scripture, 1st John 4:4, that states, *"Ye are of God, little children, and have overcome them: because greater is he that is in you, than he that is in the world."* This means that, since God is in us, no one has the power to stop us. Our job is to stay on track and focus on Him when things get tough. He will never leave us alone. Deuteronomy 31:8 states, *"And the Lord, He it is that doth go before thee; He will be with thee; He will not fail thee, neither forsake thee: fear not, neither be dismayed."* God always keeps His promises. Even when we fall short and make mistakes, He is ready, willing, and able to forgive us. All we have to do is confess our sins and ask for forgiveness. Failing to do this is essentially leaving the problem unresolved.

I have found that pleasing God and trusting Him has added enormous benefits to my life. As I go forth doing my daily chores, I ask Him to guide me through various encounters. He allows me to meet people who are kind and compassionate. Difficult situations seem to go much better than before. Proverbs 3:5-6 states, *"Trust in the Lord with all thine heart; and lean not unto thine own understanding."* We simply do not have all the answers. "In all thy ways acknowledge him, and he shall direct thy paths." While we do not know what lies ahead, we do realize that He is already there. Sometimes we view things from a narrow perspective. Many times, we fail to see how a particular problem can be resolved. We must remember that nothing is too difficult for God. He is the greatest problem solver. There is a song by Smokie Norful that says, "Even when I don't understand, I trust His plan."

We all have problems we cannot solve. I am over-joyed at how prayer can relieve stressful situations. Usually, I get an answer that I had not considered previously. I think to myself, "I would never have thought of that." The power of the Holy Spirit is awesome. Do not be afraid to tap into this powerful avenue. Sometimes, we need to explore different possibilities. Here is a simple exercise: Sit back, relax and allow your mind to be free. Next, think of different approaches to the problem. Allow yourself to stretch your imaginations; "What if I had tried this or that?" Give your subconscious a chance to work for you. You will likely be pleased with the results. I have found that stepping away from the situation is great. Maybe, I will go for a walk or listen to music. This gives the subconscious time to search for a solution. The brain works like a computer. We need to give it time to search through stored information

FAITHFULNESS

Hebrews 11:1 states, *"Now faith is the substance of things hoped for, the evidence of things not seen."* Faith is not wondering what God can do. We must believe that He can do all things. Even when we fall short in various areas of our lives, God is still faithful. He has promised never to leave or forsake us. He always comes through for us. He is the same yesterday, today and forever more: He does not change. We live in a changing world. There is comfort in knowing that He remains the same.

You may feel discouraged sometimes. Try reading the scriptures on faith. For example, the story of Abraham and Isaac. This shows, even when you do not fully understand, you can trust His plan. There is a song which says, "Great is thy faithfulness." *"Also, His loving kindness toward us"*. We cannot fully comprehend these two things. We all make mistakes. All of us get knocked down from time to time. The good news is that we can get back up again. Our trials happen to make us stronger. Once you overcome a problem; you are in a position to help someone else!

God wants to participate in our lives. He has given us free will. Therefore, we have to invite Him to be a part of our plans. He is a gentleman, and will not just barge in. He has given us the ability to make choices. Ultimately, this is our responsibility. We are in charge of our personal goals. However, choosing God as our partner is the best solution. He is able to take us to places that we never dreamed would be possible. Ephesians 3:20 states, *"Now unto him that is able to do exceeding abundantly above all that we ask or think, according to the power that worketh in us."* This means He will always exceed our expectations. Who would not want to serve a God like that?

Faith allows us to access what grace has already provided. Complaining, crying, moaning and groaning will not help. Fasting and praying is a much better option. This allows us to slow down and really hear God. One day, I was complaining to my mother. She answered, *"Stop fussing and start trusting."* This was great advice. Almost and/or no one has ever complained their way to success. Here is one of my favorite prayers. "Lord, I am your child, standing on your promises. I need your help right now. I cannot do this on my own." When we humble ourselves and ask Him for help, He will surely answer. The problem may be big or small. Just believe He can deliver us from them al

Staying Positive

Surround yourself with positive people. Make sure you have a good support system. My former pastor, Reverend, Doctor, Jim Holley, had a saying, *"Some people are headed nowhere, and they want to take you with them."* Do not allow this to happen! As stated previously, "What we think about we bring about." Hence, it is important to surround yourself with people with similar goals and values. They will help motivate you. Those who have not discovered their vision or purpose cannot help you. Stay clear of them! Join networking groups with similar goals. They will help you to remain on track. There is a saying, *"Once you make a commitment, the universe will rise up to meet you."* You will meet people on your journey who are willing to assist you. I have found this to be true. After I had made a decision, I started to meet people who were able to help me. I am amazed at how this works.

Remember to count your blessings. Do not waste time dwelling on what you do not have! Spend your time thanking God for what you do have! No matter what you are going through, continue to praise him. He has the power to pour you out blessings that you will not have room enough to contain. 2nd Corinthians 9:8 states, *"And God is able to make all grace abound toward you; that ye, always having all sufficiency in all things, may abound to every good work."* You may not believe this. I dare you to try it. What do you have to lose? Sometimes we are waiting on God to do something. While He is waiting for us to show that we have faith and commitment. You have probably heard the song entitled, "You Will Win." *"Everything attached to you will win. It's your winning season"*. You can always count on God. We must do our part. He may only perform a miracle if you are willing to participate. Ask yourself, "What can I do to be a part of my success? What can I do to assure myself of a successful outcome?" Remember you have the power to reach your destiny!

NOTES:

Chapter 5

WATCH GOD PROVIDE

Tamela Mann has a song entitled, "Watch God Provide." Go to YouTube and listen to the lyrics. This song really speaks about how God provides. She sings, *"Why do I worry about my life when you have come to my rescue a thousand times?"* Have you ever been in a difficult situation? Maybe you could not see any way out. So, you started to pray, and you thought it was all over. There did not seem to be an answer! God stepped in and worked it out. He gave you an answer that you could not come up with on your own. A lot of people rely on Google for answers. While Google is a good tool, which provides a lot of information, God is the only One with all power. He sees all and knows all.

God is in the blessing business. Genesis 3:9, *"Every moving thing that liveth shall be meat for you; even as the green herb have I given you all things."* Pastor, Reverend, Doctor, Larry Jordan once said, *"Do not focus on your needs, but rather on God's supply."* Think about it, if God has promised to supply all of your needs in His word. We know that He keeps His word. We can be confident in focusing on His supply. He has an unlimited supply. He can meet all our needs at the same time. No one else can do that. Mark 16:19, *"So then after the Lord had spoken unto them, he was received up into heaven, and sat on the right hand of God."* Christ Jesus is seated at the right hand of the father, and He works on our behalf. He gave His life for us. He is still working on our behalf. What an extraordinary blessing! This is God's mercy and grace in action! He loves us unconditionally. He continues to bless us over and over again. Trust and believe and expect great results!

There may be times when you feel lost and confused. Maybe you cannot feel God's presence. This is a good time to pray and read the scriptures. I have a promise book which breaks down various situations. This is a good thing to have in times of trouble. You can go directly to what you need. God's word is powerful and comforting. This will definitely ease your pain.

Know that He is the ultimate provider. When everything else fails, He will be right there. Recently, I had bad pain in my left hand. I could not bend my thumb. A friend was telling me how she used crystals and stones. I remembered how my grandmother used to heat bricks for arthritis. I picked up a stone off the ground while riding my bike. I heated the stone on top of the stove. This relieved the pain right away. I could bend my thumb again. What a great solution. I did not have to go to CVS or Walgreens. My grandmother did not have access to Google, but she had God. Google may be good, but God is the best.

WE HAVE NOT BECAUSE WE ASK NOT

Luke 6:38: *"Give, and it shall be given unto you; good measure, pressed down, and shaken together, and running over, shall men give into your bosom. For with the same measure that ye mete withal it shall be measured to you again."* Are you trying to launch a business? Give away some free product to those who are less fortunate. The more you give, the more you will receive. This does not just apply to money and things. You may give advice, time or other talents. The rewards will be greater than you expect. They will come in different forms. For example, I called into a radio show to congratulate them on their anniversary. They were having a celebration. The host gave me a free ticket. While I freely gave a compliment, without any expectation, I received a free ticket to the event. Hence, we reap what we sow. Sowing cheaply will bring cheap rewards. Remember whatever you give that is what you will get back. So, give freely and get great rewards! We cannot beat God in giving.

Do you want a great idea? Just ask God, He will surely answer. I am trying to launch a scarf business. There are plenty of scarves everywhere. How do I distinguish my product? God has directed me to the pet market. Also, the college football bookstores. There aren't any scarves in the bookstores. What a great idea. I was overwhelmed. I started to think what if they say yes. "How would I fill the order?" I had to remind myself that it was not my job to move the mountain. My job was to start moving toward the mountain. God is the one who can move the mountain. Sometimes He may not move the mountain. However, He can lead you all around it.

Perhaps you are in a difficult situation. Maybe you do not see a way out. Remember God may not take you out of the situation. He may choose to go through the situation with you. Either way, He is willing and able to see you through it. Writing helps to remind me of these facts. We need to pray daily to communicate with God. He will never fail you. He has rescued me many times. What major obstacles or mountains are you facing? Remember, God can help you overcome them!

CORE VALUES

Do what you know is right. You will never have any regrets. There will be no wondering, was it correct? I practice telling the truth because it is the right thing to do. Plus, it is just too hard to remember a bunch of lies. This is a good way to attract positive things into your life. Doing the opposite will bring negative things to you. This is by design. God has given us good fundamental rules to follow. They will bring us good things. While we may all get off track, this will surely happen. There is a song that says; "Trust God and come on back." The definition of integrity is firm adherence to a code of especially moral or artistic values, incorruptible. Let's say an apple is rotten to the core. You cannot eat it. The same is true with your value system. Treat others the way you want to be treated. Whatever you give, that is what you will get back. This is a good way to improve your life. Remember you have the power to make your situation better.

The true measure of one's character is how they handle adversities. We can all manage quite well when things are going smoothly. However, when trouble comes, we often lose our cool. A strong prayer life will help you get through difficult times. As the song goes, He may not come when you want Him. God is always on time. I find that when I have exhausted all possible solutions, He shows up; just as I am about to give up. I find this to be so wonderful.

According to Pastor Larry Jordan, *"Wisdom is applying God's word to your life."* He has addressed every possible situation. Many of us hear the word and know the word. However, we fail to apply it to our lives. For example, working with a computer, sometimes, it will instruct you to strike a key. You must strike it in order to complete the prompt. So, it is with our lives. You have to practice applying the word to your personal situation. Failing to do so will cause you to miss many blessings.

Ezekiel 3:10 states, *"Moreover He said unto me, Son of man, all my words that I shall speak unto thee receive in thine heart and hear with thine ears."* This means that we hear with our ears, but we should receive the word in our hearts. Once we do this, it will be easy to apply it to our lives. Also, Proverbs 22:17-18 states, *"Bow down thine ear, and hear the words of the wise, and apply thine heart unto my knowledge. For it is a pleasant thing if thou keep them within thee, they shall withal be fitted in thy lips."* These verses tell us that it is not enough to just hear the word, we must receive it in our hearts. After we receive it in our hearts, we will be able to apply it. Once you accept the word into your heart, it will freely flow from your lips. Whatever you are facing, try reading the bible. There is always a scripture to minister to your every need. Do not take my word for it! Try it for yourself. You will find this to be the best available prescription. God can fix whatever ails you. He can do it better than anyone else.

CONNECTION

Having a connection with God is critical. As individuals, we can choose whatever works for our particular situations. Some may choose going to a physical building as a way of connecting with God. Others might select the internet, television or some other media. The important thing is that you make the connection. Google defines soul as the spiritual or immaterial part of a human being or animal regarded as immortal; the essence of embodiment of a specified quality. We are body, mind, and spirit. Since God is a spirit, we need a divine connection to communicate with Him. Tapping into this vast and wonderful resources is just great. There is a song which says we are spiritual beings having a natural experience. Feeding our souls is absolutely essential.

According to God's word, we have been given authority, dominion, and power. This includes the entire earth. Many times, we fail to utilize the power we have been given. We have control over our personal decisions. Let's say you are having trouble deciding what to do. God is ready, willing and able to help you. All you have to do is ask. I have found that consulting with Him early on is the best way. This can help you avoid many pitfalls. Why not tap into this valuable resource? No matter what you are trying to accomplish, He is able and willing to assist you. Sometimes we are overwhelmed by the big picture. Remember to break your project down into small manageable steps. Review and enjoy your progress. Celebrate each small victory. This will give you the stamina to keep going.

Just take it, one day at a time. Develop a definite plan and stick to it. Making progress is a great motivator. This will add a sense of purpose and meaning to your life. A sense of hope will replace anxiety and stress. Calmly and directly, you will move toward your goals. Your thought process will change. You will declare, "Yes, I can." A positive attitude will emerge. You will have delight and pleasure as you pursue your objectives. You will sense that winning is possible.

John 15: 7 states, *"If ye abide in me, and my words abide in you, ye shall ask what ye will, and it shall be done unto you."* This is the best formula for success. Surrender your life to God. Believe and trust in Him and see how this will enrich your life. I cannot think of a better way to relieve stress. This will not cost you any money. Why do we struggle and deal with drama in our lives? There is a beautiful alternative available to everyone. God does not discriminate. He sent His Son to die for the whole world. Failing to use your God-given power is a mistake. There is a song which says; "When Jesus says yes, nobody can say no." Only He can make a way out of no way. He can turn defeat into victory. No one else has that power!

I AM THE WAY

John14:6 states, *"Jesus saith unto him, I am the way, the truth, and the life: No man cometh unto the Father, but by me."* Jesus gave

His life so that we could be saved and have eternal life. All we have to do is acknowledge this fact. Accept Him as our personal Lord and Savior. After doing this, we become a part of His family. The benefits and privileges are simply enormous. You cannot get them from anyone else. When you buy a product with a guarantee, many times the manufacturer defaults. But God never reneges on His promises. We can stand on His word and His promises. According to His word, He will never leave or abandon us.

There is a song by Richard Smallwood entitled, *"Jesus the Center of My Joy." The lyric says, "Without God, there would be no life. Don't be dead on the inside but let God in your soul and be born again. Come to life, be born again. Come to Christ"*! There is a commercial advert that says, *"Things go better with Coke."* I dare to say --- things go better with God. Choosing to surrender to God is ultimately the best. Focus on Him at the beginning of the day. You will be amazed at how great everything will go. Allow Him to be the center of your joy. No one else can give you peace and calm in the middle of a storm. When drama and stress try to invade your being, turn your attention to God and watch them disappear. He is simply majestic.

DO NOT THINK SMALL

Do not settle for less than you deserve. Do not think small. God is bigger than the universe and all of our problems. He is able to exceed our expectations. Who else can do that? Tap into His greatness. Once you submit your life to Him, all things become possible. Go for the gusto. Psalm 37:25 states,

"I have been young, and now am old; yet have I not seen the righteous forsaken, nor his seed begging bread." This gives everyone in this category unlimited opportunities. Yes, we have to do our part. He is ready, willing, and able to guide us through the process. God has an infinite supply of whatever we need. By just submitting to Him, we have access to all possible benefits. Do not wait, start using your God-given talents today!

God has given each one of us some type of talent. He wants us to use them to enrich mankind. Do not waste time withholding your contribution. Doing so will cause you to miss out on many great blessings. We are given blessings so that we can bless others. This is a part of God's design for our lives. Bring your dreams to life and reap the benefits that God has just for you. We cannot fully comprehend how much He loves us. I have personally experienced many blessings that prove this. Maybe you just do not believe it can be that simple. Try it and see! You will be pleasantly surprised.

We all face various problems. There is a song which says, "Take your burdens to the Lord and leave them there." Matthew 6:6 states, *"But thou, when thou prayest, enter into thy closet, and when thou hast shut thy door, pray to thy Father in secret; and thy Father which seeth in secret shall reward thee openly."* What a wonderful privilege. He will never disclose your business to others. That is a true blessing. He is the Most High; powerful and wonderful God!

Here are some great songs, "Wanna Be Happy," by Kirk Franklin, "The Battle Is the Lord's," and "Never Give Up," by Yolanda Adams. Listening to a good song may help you get through hard times. We all need encouragement sometimes. I have turned to friends for help a number of times. They have failed me many times. However, I can honestly say, God has never failed me. He has always given me solutions to problems, which I never dreamed were possible. Sometimes, while I am trying to figure something out, He reveals the answer, all of a sudden. He is so fantastic. Do you want a better life? Try God and expect wonderful results.

What is your dream job? How do you go about getting it? Start by consulting with God. He has all power and all the information you need. He will direct you in the path that you need to follow. While Google is a good source, He was the one who inspired man to create Google. While this can be a useful tool, God is our ultimate source. Do not fail to solicit His help. He truly wants us to have a successful and prosperous life. He has given us the provisions to ensure a positive outcome.

I find that music helps to relieve stress. I like all types of music. Gospel music is really helpful. Data shows that classical music can help you fall asleep. There is a song; "I know a place where the devil can't go. He just cannot get in." Psalm 91:1 states, *"He that dwelleth in the secret place of the Most High shall abide under the shadow of the Almighty."* Isn't it comforting to know that we can dwell in the secret place of the Most High God. He will shield us from harm and danger. The devil cannot touch us while we are under His protection. We may not know what lies ahead. We do know that He holds the future. Another song says, *"Time is in His hand, the beginning and the end. He wraps Himself in love and darkness tries to hide. All the earth rejoices and trembles at His voice"*. Why not take advantage of His magnificent power?

VISUALIZE IT UNTIL IT COMES TO PASS

Many times, your project may take longer than you anticipate. Do not get discouraged. Keep a picture visible. Look at it daily. Remind yourself it will come to life. Your hard work will pay off. Things do not happen instantly. Success involves hard work and persistence. You will eventually reap the benefits of your hard work. There is a song by Yolanda Adams, "Be still." The lyrics say, *"I told you that you could talk to me. Instead of coming to me, it's easy for you. I see to rush and get in a hurry. This causes you to be anxious and to worry. You rather do it all yourself. You know you need my help. I will never leave your side. I will never make you cry. Your best is in my hands, success is in my plans."* These lyrics are beautiful and true. What a comfort to know that God wants the best for us! He has made provisions for us to fulfill our purpose.

Romans 8:31 states, *"What shall we then say to these things? If God be for us, who can be against us?"* No one has the power to stand in your way. He will guide you through all obstacles. God is our true power source. We all encounter problems from time to time. But the key is knowing that He is larger and greater than all of our problems. Whether they are big or small, He has the power to solve them all. Whenever you are facing difficult times, lean and depend on Him. Allow Him to protect and guide you. Life will be sweeter day by day. Decide to utilize Him in your daily struggles. Watch your life reach heights that you never thought were possible. Romans 8:32 states, *"He that spared not his own Son, but delivered him up for us all, how shall he not with him also freely give us all things?"* Therefore, He truly wants us to succeed.

Do not look for approval from others. You may be disappointed many times. God is the author and finisher of your faith. Only He can take you to where you are trying to go. He is in your corner. Do not discuss your plans with everyone. They may cause you to get distracted. People may not share your plans or the vision you have for your life. So, they will not be able to encourage you. Surround yourself with positive people. Join networks with like-minded people. Stay focused on your goals. There is a song which says that God has a blessing with your name on it. Only you can claim it.

What are you trying to accomplish that may require God's help? Remember, He is always available and willing to help.

NOTES:

Chapter 6

GOD'S POWER, PROMISE, AND PURPOSE

Recently, I heard a sermon by Pastor Mario Smith. The subject was God's Power, Promise, and Purpose. We know that God has all power. Many times, we fail to tap into this unlimited provision. We spin our wheels to no avail. We need to slow down and listen to His voice. Remember, He is always with us. Know that, as the songwriter says, "He has already worked it out, while we are trying to figure it out." Romans 4:13 states, *"For the promise, that he should be the heir of the world, was not to Abraham, or to his seed, through the law, but through the righteousness of faith."* Faith is the key to the power, promise and the purpose. Faith is the vehicle that allows us to tap into these things.

We need to believe that all things are possible with God. We must start somewhere. According to Romans 8:25, which states, *"But if we hope for that we see not, then do we with patience wait for it."* Perhaps you have a picture in your mind. You can visualize the results. You do not know exactly how to accomplish your goals. However, you do know that God is able to do all things. He is working on our behalf. That is God's divine plan. God has given each of us certain talents. We must utilize them to fulfill our purpose. Decide to find out the purpose and plan He has for you. Yes, you will have to work your plan. You will replace stress with calm and serenity. No one can give us these benefits but God.

The Clark Sisters of Detroit have a song entitled, "I'm looking for a miracle." *"Believe and receive it, God can perform it today"*. Don't overthink it. Just know that God is able. He wants us to be successful. I have found this to be true, and I challenge you to try it!

THE POWER SOURCE

We have all heard the words, "God is our source." Since He has all power; this makes Him our source. Our electricity will not work unless we are connected to the power source. We must have a connection with God so that our lives will run properly. Being disconnected is not an option. Just as your home does not function without power, the same is true for your life without God. Choose to be connected to the power source. This connection is vital to our wellbeing. We may survive but for a short time lacking the power source. We must reconnect to it in order for our appliances to work. Just as food will go bad without power, the same is true of life without God. Decide to stay connected!

We will all encounter difficult times in our lives. Having a good connection with God will sustain you. Remember, no matter what you are going through, God is already there. He will never leave us on our own. We can lean and depend on Him in our darkest hours. No matter what problems we may encounter, God has the answer. Even when we cannot see the light at the end of the tunnel, He is there ready and willing to help. He does not change. He loves us unconditionally. What a wonderful thing it is to know this. Perhaps, you cannot feel His presence. Just know that you can move to His word. There is a scripture for whatever you are dealing with. He is always available. Do not fail to ask for His guidance. He knows what lies ahead of you. Therefore, He can help you get through it. His promises are secure and sure. Psalm 30:5 states, *"For his anger endureth but a moment; in his favor is life: weeping may endure for a night but joy cometh in the morning."* Going through a tough time is never easy. Sometimes, you have to praise your way through it. Remember to be thankful, no matter what you go through. There is still something to be thankful for. Even the fact that you are still here and able to feel the pain. Maybe you cannot see it as a blessing at the time. Actually, it really is. Getting through it will make you stronger and better. You have been given the opportunity to continue. God is full of grace and mercy; therefore, things will get better.

There is a song by Jessica Reedy entitled, "Better." Here are some of the words: "*I used to be so broken, lost, empty. A heart with no beat, a singer with no song to sing. I know the feeling; the silence is deafening. But in your pain lies a blessing. A sweeter song of victory. So, keep walking, walking, walking though it seems so far. no matter who you are. See there's one thing that I know, life can leave you so bitter, bitter, bitter, bitter. But you must believe it gets better, better, better, better, it's alright. Dry your eyes, send a prayer to the sky. I know it's hard to fight. But you must believe it gets better. Listen to me. I know you are scared; your heart is bleeding. But what are you gonna do now? I think --- it's time you broke free! Keep walking, walking, walking, though it seems so far. No, it doesn't matter who you are.... I was almost taking. I wanted to die from how I was doing wrong. I cried every night, looking for a helping hand. That's when it happened. Jesus took me in. He held me close, gave me love, refilled my heart, helped me grow. Better because His love made me whole. He's available anytime. Try Him out. He'll change your life".* I cannot think of a better solution.

DO NOT COMPLAIN

We all have days where nothing seems to go right. Try to find some positive feature about it. Thank God that you are alive and have an opportunity to make it better. Do not forget that no one and nothing stays the same. There is a song which says that my good days will outweigh my bad days. God has been good to me; therefore, I won't complain. When you get the urge to complain, try the following; practice being grateful and thankful for whatever you have. You cannot do both things simultaneously. I believe that being thankful and grateful is more beneficial than complaining. There is a saying, "Your attitude helps to promote your altitude." Staying positive will help your wellbeing in all areas of your life. So, choose to utilize this option.

The dictionary defines hope as the feeling of expectation and desire for a certain thing to happen. Also, aspiration, desire, wishful expectation, ambition, aim, goal, plan, design. We hope things will turn out for the best. Many times, we are disappointed. As Jessie Jackson says, "Keep hope alive."

Faith is believing in things that we cannot see. Just because you are unable to see it does not mean that it is impossible. All things are possible for those who trust and believe in God. Brian Courtney Wilson has a song, "Trust Him with your yes." You will never be disappointed. You will likely be rewarded. Trusting and obeying Him will cause blessings to flow your way. His word is true; He will pour you out blessings that are much greater than what you thought was possible. This will certainly bring you excitement.

Lamentations 3:22 states, *"It is of the Lord's mercies that we are not consumed because his compassions fail not."* This is a wonderful thing to be aware of. His compassion will never fail. Verse 23 says, *"They are new every morning: great is thy faithfulness."* I don't think we can truly comprehend this fact. Every single day, He extends new mercies. No one else can do this. He is so compassionate. This is a beautiful blessing. Do not take it for granted. Remember to be thankful!

Psalm 68:19 talks about His blessings. It says, *"Blessed be the Lord, who daily loadeth us with benefits, even the God of our salvation."* Many of us experience this daily. Sometimes we fail to realize that God is truly our provider. Recently, I went to the mall to get my eyebrows arched. The eyebrow lady was on break. I decided to go into Sears. I found a pair of leggings that I really liked. I asked the sales clerk to check my point status. I was very surprised to find out that I had enough points to satisfy the bill. What a joy to receive an unexpected blessing. Next, I proceeded to get my eyebrows done. The lady ahead of me pulled out a gift card to pay for her service. This reminded me that I had the same card in my wallet. I did not have to pay for my eyebrow service. I was very grateful. His works are so marvelous. Sometimes we think it is a coincidence. I know that is how He works in our everyday life. God is truly a wonder!

DO NOT WAIT

Start now, do not wait! It may get too late. There is a song by Deborah Joy Winans, "The Master's Calling." Here are the lyrics; "Listen, while you still can hear. The master's calling. Bow down while your knees still bend. The master is calling. I don't want to run or walk away from him. Bind me to your side. Seek him though your eyes don't see. The master is calling. Praise him while your lips still sing. The master is calling." There is an urgency to this song. Also, this is true of our lives. Do not procrastinate; start now! This will give you a sense of purpose and meaning. Your efforts will bring great benefits. They may not happen immediately. Just know they will come forth.

Bow down while your knees still bend. Communicate with God while you have the chance. There is a saying; "Yesterday is gone, tomorrow may not come; right now is all we have." Do not fail to utilize it fully. This song truly touched my spirit on many levels. Seek him though your eyes don't see. John 4:24 tells us that God is a spirit and they that worship him must worship him in spirit and truth. Even though we can't see him, we have to believe and trust that he really does exist. According to Google and Webster, the definition of spirit is the nonphysical part of a person that is the seat of emotions and character, the soul. A supernatural being or essence: as a capitalized, holy spirit: the soul is an often malevolent being that is bodiless but can become visible: ghost: a malevolent being that enters and possesses a human being.

We can all apply this song to our personal goals. We need to start now, do not wait another minute. There is an urgency of fulfilling your purpose. The sooner you get started, the better. There is no need to wait; tomorrow may be too late.

There is a saying; we should live each day as if it is our last. Steve Jobs embraced this philosophy. He said that someday, it would be true. Act as if you may not have another chance. Make your purpose your top priority. What could be more important than that? The master is calling. He has given each of us an assignment. So, I urge you to start carrying it out today. Dare to step into your destiny. There is a blessing with your name on it. Do not allow it to go unclaimed. What is the master calling you to do? Do not procrastinate!

WHAT REALLY MATTERS

Most of us have heard the saying; "Only what you do for Christ will last." I once heard a sermon stating we could choose to leave this world with Christ as our Savior. Even though we came into this world with nothing, and we will not take anything with us, Christ is the only exception. What a wonderful and beautiful gift for mankind. I once heard someone say, "It will not matter if you have a Ph.D., at the end of life, it will only matter if you have GOD." We will be judged by how we treated one another. God has given us certain principles to live by. Decide to utilize them. This will help you live a better life.

Psalm 39:6 reads as follows, *"Surely every man walketh in a vain shew: surely they are disquieted in vain: he heaps up riches, and knoweth not who shall gather them."* I have bought many items because they were on sale. There was no real need for them. Many times, I have given them as gifts. The recipient was happy as a result. Both parties benefited from the purchases. Perhaps, this is how it was meant to be. I really believe it is better to give than to receive. There is a joy that comes with giving.

I remember smoking a turkey for Christmas a few years ago. I did not realize at the time why. A friend of mine had a relative to pass. I was able to give the family most of the turkey. God always knows what lies ahead. I believe He gives us the instinct to prepare for things before they occur. I am amazed at how this works. He is the God who knows everything. There is a song which says; "There is no one greater than Him." What a powerful God we serve!

Accept whatever assignment He has for you. Do not put it off. Make a commitment to start now. You will have peace beyond anything you can imagine. Jesus Christ is the greatest gift of all. John 3:16 states, *"For God so loved the world, that he gave his only begotten Son, that whosoever believeth in him should not perish, but have everlasting life."* According to Pastor Larry Jordan, receiving the gift is only part of the process. You must open the gift in order to receive the benefits. Leaving it in the box will not give you any consolation. You must open it and apply it to your personal situation. Only then will you receive the many benefits God has to offer. God wants to be an innate part of our lives. However, we must accept Him as our personal Savior for that to happen. We all have a choice and a voice in our personal lives. There were some soap operas entitled, "All My Children, One Life to Live, and Another world." We are all His children. We have one life to live. We should, therefore, choose to live for God. He will surely take us to another world.

THAT WAS NOT THE ANSWER I EXPECTED

Many times, we pray, but we do not get the answer we expect. Sometimes, the answer may simply be no. Those who have children can relate to this. The answer is not always yes. Occasionally, you have to say no. So, it is with God. Maybe you prayed hard for a loved one to recover, but they did not. The answer was simply no. You had to suffer their loss. While this is quite painful, we are all born to die. Psalm 100:3 states, *"Know ye that the Lord is God: it is he that hath made us, and not we ourselves; we are his people, and the sheep of his pasture."* We all belong to Him; therefore, He can take us whenever He chooses.

Job 13: 15 explains it this way, *"Though he slay me, yet will I trust him: but I will maintain mine own ways before him."* Job lost almost everything, but he still trusted God. God gave him back more than he had: Job 42:10 declares this fact. We may not understand why we are going through a particular situation. Proverbs 3: 5 says, *"Trust in the Lord with all thine heart; and lean not unto thine own understanding."* Even though we don't understand, we can always trust Him. Just as He gave Job twice as much as he had before, so will He do for us.

Greatly was Job rewarded because of his faithfulness. No matter what you are going through, trust God. There is hope for tomorrow because He lives. There is a song by Cece Winans, "Great is thy faithfulness." We may not always get the answer we want. God still provides. God is still good. He never fails. Even in the midst of a storm, He can calm the raging sea. Therefore, He will surely take care of you and me. He will never let go of us. He has promised to be with us always. Psalm 23: 4 says, *"Yea, though I walk through the valley of the shadow of death, I will fear no evil: for thou art with me; thy rod and thy staff they comfort me."* Remember God is ready, willing, and able to comfort us. He can give us peace and joy in spite of the storm. He will be with us forever.

GOD OUR REDEEMER

God is our Redeemer. Psalm 103:4 states the following, *"Who redeemeth thy life from destruction, who crowneth thee with loving kindness and tender mercies."* Even when we are disobedient, He is still merciful and kind. He continues to bless us over and over again. He loves us with no conditions. Psalm 23: 6 confirms God's love. *"Surely goodness and mercy shall follow me all the days of my life and I will dwell in the house of the Lord forever."* We can expect goodness and mercy our entire lives. We can expect to spend eternity with God. What a mighty and wonderful God we serve. We may not have everything that we want; life is still worth living. Things may not be perfect. Remember to be thankful for whatever you have. Just as the song says, you must believe it will get better. Romans 8:28 states, *"And we know that all things work together for good to them that love God, to them who are called according to his purpose."* Therefore, we must get busy fulfilling our purpose. This will bring blessings beyond our expectations.

There is a song by Casey J. called, "I'm yours." Here are some of the words. *"We belong to you, Lord. I'm yours, have all of me. Your song flows through my lips. Your work moves through my hands. Your thoughts stay on my mind. Your love lives in my heart. Have all of me"*. When we surrender to God, He will direct our path. There is nothing better than embracing His love. There are endless benefits that await us. Submitting to His will is a wonderful thing. There is nothing more rewarding than watching the hand of God move in our lives. Your life will have a purpose and more meaning. You will manage stress calmly and with ease. Can you think of anything that can make life any better than that?

There is a scripture that advises us thus; the spirit is willing, but the flesh is weak. Matthew 26:41 says, *"Watch and pray, that ye enter not into temptation: the spirit indeed is willing, but the flesh is weak."* For example, many times you may plan to run a list of errands on a given day. However, physically, you are not able to complete them as planned. Therefore, the spirit was willing, but the body was not able to comply. You must work while you have the energy. Take full advantage of this resource, while it is available. Usually, it is not the same all the time. You must seize the moment. Sometimes, I am able to write most of the day. I have to take the opportunity while it is there. This does not happen every day. My aunt, Mary, used to say; *"Be sure to do what you can, while you can."* Remember energy and time are limited items.

A CHOICE AND A VOICE

We all have a choice and a voice regarding life. How we choose to use it is totally up to us. We must take responsibility for our actions. Therefore, we should use wisdom upon making decisions. Including God in the process early on is a wise choice! He knows all and sees all! Who else would be a better consultant? As previously stated, Google has a lot of information; only God has all the information. He gives it to us freely. All we have to do is ask. James 1:5 states the following, *"If any man lack wisdom, let him ask of God, that giveth to all men liberally, and upbraideth not; and it shall be given him."* I have often wondered what the word upbraideth meant. According to Webster, it means to criticize severely: find fault with. God does not judge us for not knowing. He wants us to lean and depend on Him. What a wonderful Father He is to all of His children. This verse informs us that He does not discriminate. What a marvelous blessing this is for those who believe.

There is a Gaelic proverb which says there are three types of people. Those who make things happen, those who watch things happen, and those who wonder at what happens. Each one of us can choose the one we want to be. Ask yourself,

"What can I do to make things happen in my life." Do not waste time moaning and complaining, get busy making your life better. God has given us power and authority over the entire earth. Use it, do not allow the enemy to rob you of your dreams. There is a song by Ernest Pugh, entitled; "Show Me Your Glory, Show Me Your Power." The song also says, "*I need your glory, I need your power. More of you and less of me.*" When we allow God to work through us, we can accomplish great things. He is able to take us places beyond our wildest dreams. I am so amazed at how I always get more than I expect. I realize that this does not happen by my own power. Allowing God to work through you will yield incredible results. Which type of person do you wish to be? Remember you have the power to make that choice.

NOTES:

Chapter 7

WAIT ON THE LORD

James 1:3-4 says, *"Knowing this, that the trying of your faith worketh patience. But let patience have her perfect work, that ye may be perfect and entire, wanting nothing."* Many times, we need to be patient and wait on the Lord. As the saying goes, "Haste makes waste." There is a song by Donnie McClurkin entitled, "Wait on the Lord." Here are some of the words. *Sometimes in life, you'll find that you get in a hurry. But when you have assurance no need to worry. You can wait, wait, wait on the Lord. You'll see that he always keeps his word. You must just trust in him. Don't be dismayed. Patience in times of trouble, trust and believe him. Everything God promised you will receive... Wait on the Lord, be of good courage. Wait and he will strengthen your heart.* Maybe you are going through a tough time, try listening to this song and praying. Sometimes praise and worship can help you get through a difficult situation. This may lift your spirit and ease the pain.

EMPOWERING THE NEXT GENERATION

I believe God wants us to use our talents to empower the next generation. I have started a scarf business. I have decided to teach young girls how to make scarves. Perhaps I will get an order that I cannot fill alone. They will be trained to help me.

God gives us talents so that we can help others. He did not intend for us to go through life's journey alone. All of us have a rich heritage to share with others. Therefore, we need to share our gifts. Use your gifts and talents to help empower the next generation.

I believe God wants us to use our talents to bless others. I believe God blesses us so that we can be a blessing. This is how it has been designed. Luke 12:48 says, *"But, he that knew not, and did commit things worthy of stripes, shall be beaten with few stripes. For unto whomsoever much is given, of him shall be much required: and: and to whom men have committed much, of him they will ask the more."* This is a good way to pass on your God-given talents. Also, you will be helping to empower the next generation. I believe this skill may help some young person get through a tough time. This is how the spirit of God works. We are body, mind, and spirit. God speaks to our spirits. *"We must worship him in spirit and truth,"* John 4:23-24 admonishes us. He wants us to help others.

There is a Chinese Proverb which says, *"Give a man a fish, and you feed him for a day, teach him to fish, and you give him skill for life."* We need to apply this idea to our daily lives. There are millions of retired people in the United States. Their talents should not be wasted. Maybe you are guilty of not utilizing your God-given talents. Let's say you are retired and not contributing to society. You have the ability to change. Some may say, "I worked hard all my life. I really don't want to do anything." I'm sure you have heard the adage, *"We were created to wear out, not to rust out."* Helping others will give you so much fulfillment. You will likely gain much more than you give. The Bible states that it is more blessed to give than to receive (Acts 20:35). Don't take my word for it. Try it for yourself and watch what happens. I predict you will get tremendous results!

There is a Gaelic Proverb which states; *"The hand that gives gets."* Scripture says in Acts 20:35, *"I have shewed you all things, how that so laboring ye ought to support the weak, and to remember the words of the Lord Jesus, how He said, "It is more blessed to give than to receive."* Practice this principle and watch your territory increase. God is truly the ultimate provider. Reverend, Doctor Jim Holley used to say, *"God will never give you a vision without making provisions."* I have found this to be true. I cannot think of anything better to do than empowering the next generation!

LETTING GO

We all get stuck sometimes and find it difficult to move. Often, we find ourselves stuck in undesirable situations. I heard Mary J. Blige say, *"I had to leave in order to save myself."* Maybe that is the case with you. Yet, you feel stuck. You cannot leave. The relationship is not meeting your needs. Still, you keep holding on and holding out. You may be meeting a need for a person; however, he or she is not doing the same for you. Against all odds, you are hopeful that things will work out. You keep hoping and praying, but it does not change. Deep down, you know it is time to move on. You wonder why you can't find peace. Ask yourself, "What is best for me?" Answer the question! Make a decision and execute it. According to Bruce and Cheryl Bickel, Stan and Karin Jantz, authors of "Life's Little Handbook of Wisdom," a decision may not get easier with delay. Most likely, the opposite will happen. The longer you put it off, the harder it gets.

Praying and fasting will help you remain focused. Ask God to direct your path. He will surely show you the way. He is your ultimate guide. He can help you get through anything. Trust and believe it will get better. Trials and misfortunes help us to become stronger. We learn from the hard lessons of life. I believe God wants us to enjoy all phases of our lives. Many times, we have to simply let it go and let God come. You will experience peace. Eventually, you will get something much better. How do I know this, you may ask? This has happened to me many times. That is how God operates. I really cannot explain it. I just know that is how it works.

For example, it is good to clean out our closets. We need to get rid of old clothes and things. It's a job that most hate to tackle. Yet, most will admit that after it is completed, there is a good feeling. Rooms are made for new clothing, and the old clothing becomes a blessing for someone else. Thus, the process of giving becomes God's plan to bless the giver.

THE BALCONY VERSUS THE FRONT ROW

Sometimes people want to keep you in the balcony. Remember God has created you to be in the front row. Do not allow anyone to place you in the balcony. You are in control of your destiny. God has created you to be the head and not the tail.

Deuteronomy 28:13 says; *"And the Lord shall make thee the head, and not the tail; and thou shall be above only, and thou shalt not be beneath; if that thou hearken unto the commandments of the Lord thy God, which I command thee this day, to observe and to do them."* God's word is true; you can believe what it says.

You must take control and move toward your goals. Learn to manage the resources that God gives you. He gives each of us talents and potential. Do not fail to utilize what you have been given. You have a responsibility to yourself and mankind. You were created to fulfill your dreams. Your job is to get busy doing it. You will experience a sense of calmness. Life will have more meaning. You will have more confidence as you strive to reach greater heights. Christ came so that we could have a more abundant life. That means God wants us to enjoy all dimensions of our lives. Do not allow the enemy to cheat you out of what God has promised you. Vow to experience all the goodness and grace that God has to offer.

FORGIVENESS

Dealing with hurt feelings and bruised egos can be a difficult thing. They can cause us to get stuck in the wrong place. Do not waste time trying to retaliate. Yes, it is OK to vent, but complaining to others is not the answer. Try talking to God. He can truly help you get through the process. We really need His help in this situation. The normal reaction is to strike back. Remember, you may try to correct others, but only God can change their hearts. Work on a way to forgive them. You do not want to remain stuck. This will harm your creativity and your productivity. Holding on to a grudge will only harm you. Forgiveness is for your wellbeing. This may be easier said than done! Retaliation feels good sometimes! Yet, I have found that it is never worth the effort. Forgiveness will help you heal and move on with your life. Your time and energy will be better spent on accomplishing your goals. Romans 12:19 says, *"Vengeance is mine. I will repay said the Lord."* God forgives us, so He expects us to forgive others.

There's a song by Tina Campbell entitled, "Forgiveness." The words are quite powerful. *"Maybe you feel entitled because this should have never ever happened to you. Maybe you have tried to let go but letting go just ain't never easy to do. Maybe you feel you will end up with another broken heart. Trying to face something that seems way too hard. But it's too hard to hold on to all of the pain. It's too hard to relive it over and over again. It's too hard when the memories have control over you. Some say it's too hard to forgive; I say it's too hard not to. Lord help me to forgive because it's too hard not to..."* God is able to help us to do what seems impossible".

I have found that helping others is good therapy. It takes your mind off of your problems. Thinking of ways to assist someone else will help to free your mind. Also, this will make you feel better. Positive thinking is good for the soul. Coming up with a plan will likely give you relief. Putting a plan into action will help you to move forward. Your problem may not go away. However, this will keep you from being stuck in the past. Hopefully, in time, you will be able to put the situation behind you. Ultimately, you want to reach a state where positive thoughts will flow through you. Returning to focus on your goals will benefit you and others. Are you having trouble with letting go and forgiveness?

NOTES:

Chapter 8

WANT MORE DO MORE

Perhaps you are wondering how to have a more abundant life. Here are some suggestions. Start by having a more inmate relationship with God. Just as with your other personal relationships, you must invest time and effort. The same goes for God. Make time for Him daily. You will never regret it. Things may go better with others. Well, they really go better with God. Start your day by talking to Him. Do not just ask Him what you want Him to do for you, but rather how you can serve Him. You will be amazed at the results. You will likely be blessed beyond your imagination.

The best way to get more is to do more. Just as with personal relationships, the more you give, the more you will receive. God wants a deep and personal relationship with us. The more we develop this, the more benefits we will receive. Try using your talents to help others. You will receive blessings and benefits that you never thought were possible. This is a good formula for success. Remember God wants to be involved in every part of our lives. I believe we miss many benefits by not allowing this to happen. According to Joyce Meyers, one of the best things for whatever ails us is the following. "Trust God and do Good." Remember, He is always available to aid you. You are never alone.

CLOSING AND OPENING DOORS

God is able to close doors that no man can open and open doors that no man can close. Revelation 3:8 states, *"I know thy works: behold, I have set before thee an open door, and no man can shut it: for thou hast a little strength, and hast kept my word, and hast not denied my name."* We serve a God who has all power. No one can overrule Him. For example, you may be struggling with something difficult. You can't seem to find a solution. Remember, God is greater than all of your problems. Allow Him to guide you through them. He is ready, willing, and able to assist you. All you have to do is ask. Sit back and watch the wonderful results. While He may not get rid of the obstacles you may be facing, He can open up an avenue that you never even considered in your wildest dreams. He may not eliminate your problem. But He can certainly show you how to overcome it. His word says, "I have set before thee an open door." This means He can put you in a position to succeed against all odds. Therefore, no one will be able to stop you. We do not have the strength to do it on our own, but He can help us reach our destination. He wants to be a part of all elements of our lives.

Ephesians 2:8 says, *"For by grace are ye saved through faith; and not of yourselves: it is the gift of God."* We are surrounded by God's goodness and mercy daily. Many times, we are too busy to enjoy it. Do you really want to reap the benefits of this tremendous power? Perhaps you need to slow down and enjoy the beauty of a given moment. Go for a walk and take the time to embrace His marvelous creation. Do not forget to thank Him for allowing you this opportunity. There are many that wish they could trade places with you. Do not take your health and wellbeing for granted. Live in the present. Don't worry about the past or the future. Take advantage of what is before you right now. I believe that you will be pleasantly surprised.

THE POWER OF THE HOLY SPIRIT

We all have dreams and goals. We have aspirations and passion. How do we turn them into reality? Allow the Holy Spirit to guide and direct you. Ask for specific directions. He really does have all the answers. For example, I was having trouble sleeping. I decided to fast and pray. I asked for guidance and direction. I was reminded that when I stopped eating meat, I really slept better. I had forgotten about that. But God brings things to our memories for our own good.

This is one of the most valuable tools we possess. We must not fail to utilize it. This is always available and ready. Remember, we have been given power and dominion over the whole earth. Sometimes we need to be reminded of this fact. We have allowed the enemy to rob us of our God-given power. God is still in control. Therefore, we can reclaim it at any time. What a powerful God we serve. He is concerned about every part of our lives. All we have to do is acknowledge Him and ask for help. I have found that the faster I give Him the problem, the sooner it gets resolved. While I'm trying to figure it out, God has already worked it out.

John 14: 26 says to us, *"But the Comforter, which is the Holy Ghost, whom the Father will send in my name, he shall teach you all things, and bring all things to your remembrance, whatsoever I have said unto you."* We can stand on His word because it is true. His promises are certain. All we have to do is trust and believe. He will give solutions that we never imagined were possible. Allow the Holy Spirit to fuel your passion and desires.

RECEIVING GOD'S BLESSINGS

Many times, we are waiting on God to help us. However, God may be waiting for us to exercise our faith; the blessing is already ours. All we have to do is employ our faith in order to take advantage of it. On some occasions, that is the case. We may find ourselves asking God for something that He has already provided. I have been guilty of this. I had some time waited on God to reveal an idea or a solution to me. Eventually, I realized it was already available. All I needed to do was to exercise faith and receive it. This may sound too good to be true. However, it is really a fact.

God is always working on our behalf. We just need to do the work that is set before us. Sometimes, He does give us revelations. There are times when we already have what we need to complete the job. Remember, He loads us with benefits on a daily basis. Often, we fail to take advantage of what we have been given. Jesus has died for our sins, and by His stripes, we are healed. Therefore, there are blessings and all we have to do is receive them. As the song says, "Believe and receive it, God can perform it today!"

For example, whatever you are looking for is in the scriptures. Let's say you are looking for favor, simply read the scriptures pertaining to this. Apply what it says, and it is yours. Many times, we fail to apply God's word to our personal situations. We think it cannot be that simple. Do not overthink it. Just try it and see what happens!

Favor is what happens when things work out despite our performances. 1st John 3:22 states, *"And whatsoever we ask, we receive of him, because we keep his commandments, and do those things that are pleasing in his sight."* For instance, I took my sewing machine in for a tune-up. I was unable to get there early as I had planned. Still, I was able to get it done that same day. This was a case of God showing me a favor. There is a song; *"Favor ain't fair, but it sure is fabulous."*

VULNERABILITY

I read an article on vulnerability in the Wall Street Journal magazine. I thought it was worth sharing. According to Webster's dictionary, vulnerability is being easily attacked or harmed. No one wants to feel weak or uncertain. Yet, we all encounter this at certain times. Things happen that are simply out of our control. We feel helpless and unsure. Death, earthquakes, fires, hurricanes, terrorist attacks; just to name a few. These are becoming common occurrences in our world today. Ann Pasternak was quoted in the article on vulnerability stating the following. "Vulnerability could be the word for our time." She thinks if we were to name this period, it could easily be called the "Vulnerability ERA." There are people who are feeling vulnerable, insecure and fearful right now. Faith and prayer are great tools to help us manage such situations. Learn to lean and depend on God for He is always available.

You may not feel like reading the Bible during these times; however, you will be glad that you did. There is a scripture for whatever you are going through. Your problems may seem overwhelming at this moment in time. Remember nothing is too hard for God. Turning to Him in times of trouble is always beneficial. Isolation is not an answer. While friends and family may be helpful during this time, God is the ultimate helper. He is able to bring peace and calm to anyone. How we handle difficult challenges shows how strong we are.

Think of vulnerability as an opportunity to have a close encounter with God. Do not look at it as a negative thing. Remember we all encounter difficult times. How we choose to handle them is what makes the difference. God sees all of our flaws, yet He loves us unconditionally. He can still use us to fulfill His purpose in our lives. What a wonderful thing to realize this simple fact. Tavis Smiley said this, "Everyone is chasing success rather than greatness, and greatness is achieved by loving and serving others." Try applying this principle in your personal and business relationships. Jesus gave many examples of this throughout His ministry. He was always serving others. You will find these examples by reading Matthew, Mark, Luke, and John.

CRISIS AND CHALLENGES

Crisis and challenges seem to come at the most inconvenient times. Do you find yourself thinking the following? Why does this happen now? There is never a good time for trouble and strife to come. They cause us to change our plans. We have to adapt and manage the situation. However, we are never alone. God has promised to be with us always. He always keeps His promises. All we have to do is trust and believe in Him. Just as troubles seem to come suddenly and unexpectedly, so do answers from God sometimes come when we least expect them. I am surprised at how this seems to happen without warning. Tasha Cobbs has a song which states these words. *"You make my world go round when it was upside down. God is always with us even in the midst of trouble. We can count on him. He will never fail to aid us in the time of need. He is able to bring peace and calm in the midst of a storm!*

Crisis and struggles keep us humble. They remind us that God is in control. We tend to read the Bible and pray more during these times. We can find comfort and peace in His word. We are reminded that we cannot handle life's problems alone. I believe problems come to increase our faith and make us stronger. They give us the opportunity to have a deeper and closer relationship with God. We reap enormous benefits from these experiences. There is a song which tells us this testimony; "If I never had a problem, I would not know that God could solve it." There is a saying that we go through tests in order to produce testimony. The Bible tells us in 1st Peter 5: 7, *"Casting all your care upon him: for he careth for you."* I know that each time I release my problems to God, I always get amazing results.

SUBMISSION

Most of us like to think that we have a certain amount of control in our lives. The truth is, we are never really in control.

The sooner we realize this the better. I have found that submitting my entire life to God is wonderful. I no longer struggle with difficult decisions. I immediately give them to God. Maybe I just do not totally understand. I know that I can trust His plan. He knows what is best for me. You might have thought that you really wanted something, and later you discovered that it was good that you did not get it at that time. God knows exactly what we need. His timing is always perfect and precise.

He wants us to have a prosperous and productive life. We have been given authority, dominion, and power over the earth. We have a mind, soul, and body. We possess certain talents. God has a purpose for us. Our job is to discover and carry out the plan He has for us. Maybe, you are in need of direction and guidance. All you have to do is ask. He is always available and willing to help. So, get busy doing your part. He will never fail to hold up His end of the bargain.

As soon as you decide to submit to God's plan and purpose for your life, you will experience peace. Philippines 4:7 states, *"And the peace of God, which passeth all understanding, shall keep your hearts and minds through Christ Jesus."* Life will become better day by day. Giving up control can be a good thing. You will find that God will never give you misleading advice. What a blessing! Where else can you find that? Do not fail to use the Holy Spirit as your guide. I have found that there is nothing better. Submission can be a beautiful thing in many areas of your life. There may be times you want to maintain a certain amount of control over your destiny. Go for it! Do not fail to include God as your partner. You will experience a tremendous amount of benefits. How do you handle crisis and challenges? To whom do you turn in your moments of crisis and challenges?

NOTES:

About The Author

Annie P. Jones is a graduate of Madonna University. She received a Bachelor of Science degree in Business Administration in 1995 and a Master of Arts degree in English in 2014. She is a member of Family Victory Fellowship Church in Southfield, Michigan. Reverend, Doctor Larry Jordan is the pastor. She assists with the preparation of Communication. She is an occasional speaker for Christian Women events. Annie loves the Lord with all her heart and enjoys sharing the good news.

www.ingramcontent.com/pod-product-compliance
Lightning Source LLC
Chambersburg PA
CBHW052112070526
44584CB00017B/2453